D0783719

Devotions for Junior Highs

Devotions for Junior Highs

HELEN F. COUCH
and
SAM S. BAREFIELD

ABINGDON PRESS
NEW YORK—NASHVILLE

DEVOTIONS FOR JUNIOR HIGHS

Library of Congress Catalog Card Number: 60-12071

SET UP, PRINTED, AND BOUND BY
THE PARTHENON PRESS, AT NASHVILLE,
TENNESSEE, UNITED STATES OF AMERICA

Contents

A Prayer Before I Worship

O God, help me open my mind and heart to you now.

Speak to me. Let me listen well and help me to respond.

Forgive me if, in my fumbling efforts, I speak so often and so fretfully that I cannot hear you speaking to me.

And help me, whenever I speak to you, to speak truly and with pure intent.

Speak to me now, O God. Let me listen well and help me to respond.

Through Christ our Lord I pray. AMEN.

on busy, dizzy days you can . . .

Stop the Merry-Go-Round

IN THEIR SEARCH FOR BURIED CITIES AND ANCIENT roads archaeologists are making good use of aerial photography. From photographs taken in the air they can often trace the old roadways and distinguish mounds that tell of buried cities.

The entire terrain can be photographed from above and the archaeologist can then spot the signs that tell him where to dig—signs that are unrecognizable to men working on the ground where they cannot see beyond the great masses of rock or the vastness of the desert.

Have you ever felt that you had so much to do that you couldn't see where to begin digging? There is an English theme due tomorrow, a special report overdue for science class. Maybe there's a program or party you are responsible for in your church group—to say nothing of the regular tasks to be done at home and at school. And all those hours that have to be given to special practicing—music, sports, drama! And the matter of dates and keeping up with friendships too!

It's overwhelming. You feel as if you're on a fast spinning merry-go-round and that at any minute you may lose your grip on that galloping horse.

Sometimes when things crowd in on us like this our worship can become more meaningful. Whether in a daily time of private worship or the regular worship service at the church, here is our opportunity to draw aside, to rise above all these pressures. With minds and bodies quiet we can become aware of God's presence. And in his presence things that loomed so large just ahead seem to recede and grow smaller. It is as though we were looking at them from a distance.

Then we can begin to see our tasks more clearly in relation to one another. And, like the aerial photographer, we can see them in relation to the total landscape of our lives, that is, in relation to our long-range plans, our deepest purposes and dreams. The tasks that are really important stand out like the mounds in his pictures and we can trace the dim road that winds into the future. Turning our minds to God and yielding to his guidance, we can see more clearly where to "dig."

Be still, and know . . . My help comes from the Lord, who made heaven and earth. (Ps. 46:10; 121:2)

O God, help me learn to quiet my busy mind. Show me the way to still my restless body so that I may know your presence and hear you speak. AMEN.

when you have trouble . . .

Finding Out What's Right

HUCK FINN SAID, "CONSCIENCE TAKES UP MORE ROOM than all the rest of a fellow's insides!"

And sometimes you think it *does.*

Everything goes along fine. Nobody's mad at anybody. Everything is just right at school. No fusses at home. And then one day, way down deep, way down *inside,* you realize something has gone wrong.

Almost anything can get that conscience upset. Staying out later than you are supposed to . . . neglecting to tell *all* the truth . . . failing to do a job as well as you could have . . . and a lot of other things. Just fall short a bit, and suddenly you know what Huck Finn meant about conscience.

The only way to handle the unruly scoundrel is to fight him on his own grounds: see to it that he doesn't have anything to get upset about. That means trying to act on what you know to be right. And that is quite an order for anybody.

The trick is to find the principles that you want to operate on. Principles are beliefs that help us know what we ought to do, or not do. "A scout is trustworthy" —there's a principle. Here's another one: "Do good to those who hate you."

But how do you find the *right* principles? Unfortunately, they are not written out for anyone anywhere, but we do have good clues to help us find out for ourselves what the best principles are. One good place to get some help is in the gospel of Matthew in the section we call the Sermon on the Mount:

Blessed are the peacemakers, for they shall be called sons of God.

Let your light so shine before men, that they may see your good works and give glory to your Father who is in heaven.

Make friends quickly with your accuser.

If anyone strikes you on the right cheek, turn to him and other also. (MATT. 5:9, 16, 25, 39)

There are many other principles in the Sermon on the Mount. You can read them all in the fifth and sixth and seventh chapters of Matthew.

You must be wondering how on earth you can remember so many, many principles. What's the *main* thing to remember? Someone asked Jesus a question like that. Remember his answer?

"Which commandment is the first of all?"

Jesus answered, "The first is, 'Hear, O Israel: The Lord our God, the Lord is one; and you shall love the Lord your God with all your heart, and with all your soul, and with all your mind, and with all your strength.' The second is this, 'You shall love your neighbor as yourself.' There is no other commandment greater than these." (MARK 12:28-31)

So the main thing is *love*—love for God, and love for our neighbor. When we are faced with a problem, having to decide right from wrong, this is what we must remember: Whatever we do, we must do in love, to the best interest of our neighbor, and in the name of Christ.

O God, I want to learn to make all my decisions and choices as you would have me make them. I know that it will not always be easy to find the right principles; guide me—and forgive me when I make mistakes. In Jesus' name I pray. AMEN.

sometimes it seems . . .

They Just Don't Understand

"MY PARENTS JUST DON'T UNDERSTAND." HOW OFTEN have you said that to your friends? "Things are different now. It's not the same as when they were young—"

Yes, things are different, and in many ways. When your parents were your age, no one was seriously considering a trip to the moon. Color photographs of the Milky Way had never been taken. Video tape was unheard of. Jet transatlantic flights were still science fiction. Yes, many things are different.

But many things are the same too. Do you suppose your father never had any trouble getting the family car for a date? Do you really believe that nothing was ever said about what time it was when your mother came home late from a party? Are you sure they never had to do any maneuvering to get that new dress or sport coat? And their friends—surely their parents didn't always approve.

Chances are that at your age your parents went through many experiences that were much the same as yours. Perhaps they, too, often felt their parents did not understand. Could it be that they learned some things from their experiences that might help in your difficulties if they had an opportunity to share them with you? Is it possible that you do not give them a chance to understand you?

It is usually so much easier to say "they don't understand" than it is to go half way in trying to reach an understanding with anyone, even parents. And, if we're really honest with ourselves, don't we have to admit that we sometimes find a certain satisfaction in thinking we're misunderstood? This, we tell ourselves and our friends, is a reason for doing some things that do not quite square with what we know it right. This, in turn, only brings on more misunderstandings.

Today think honestly and prayerfully along these lines: When did I last feel that my parents did not understand? Did I really give them a chance to under-

stand—give them all the facts? Did I fully state my point of view and my feelings? Did I take time to listen and try to understand their point of view? How did I act—childishly? Thoughtfully? As an adult? Could we have reached a compromise that would have made us all happier?

Love is patient and kind; love is not jealous or boastful; it is not arrogant or rude. Love does not insist on its own way; it is not irritable or resentful; it does not rejoice at wrong, but rejoices in the right.

(I Cor. 13:4-6)

Forgive me when I withdraw from my problems in self-pity and childishness, Father. Help me learn to look at misunderstandings with my parents in a mature manner and try hard to work them out. Especially help me remember the love that is at the heart of my family's life and of the universe in which we live. Amen.

don't forget there's adventure . . .

In Your Own Back Yard

You have probably seen a lot of odd valentines—sweet ones, mean ones, comic ones, gooey ones. But have you ever seen one like this:

VALENTINE FOR EARTH

Oh, it will be fine
to rocket through space
and see the dark side
of the man's shadowed face,

to travel to Saturn
or Venus or Mars,
or maybe discover
some uncharted stars.

But do they have anything
better than we
possess on the earth?
Do they have a blue sea

for sailing or swimming?
Do they have hills
with raspberry thickets
where song-sparrows fill

the summer with music?
And do they have snow
to silver the roads
where schoolbuses go?

Oh, I'm all for rockets
and worlds cold or hot,
but I'm still in love
with the planet we've got! [1]

This may be a strange Valentine, but it says something important to us. Right here at our feet is an adventurous and exciting world. We may thrill when we hear about the wonders of space and feel funny inside when we read about the men who are the pioneers in space travel. But right *here,* right *now,* God gives us adventure. All our daydreaming of "somewhere else" and "another day" simply keeps us from the fun of finding out what today holds for us.

Today—is God's gift—a day full of surprises, waiting for us to tear them open and enjoy them.

Right here, wherever we are—a whirling, flaming, stirring back yard of our own, with friends to meet, ideas to explore, tasks to do, a world to be served.

And here you are now.

Remember also your Creator in the days of your youth. (Eccl. 12:1)

Take your eyes off the far away for a few moments today. Remember that God has made you for this moment, and has placed you where you are . . .

Thank him for here . . . and for now . . .

And ask him to show you the excitement in the world around you, so that you may become a part of the world that is your own back yard.

When You Are Tempted

TEMPTATION IS AS MUCH A PART OF EVERYDAY LIFE AS breathing. From the moment we open our eyes in the morning to the second when we finally lose consciousness in sleep we are continually being tempted.

Sometimes we are tempted in ways that we hardly recognize as temptation. We are tempted to be insincere in our relationships with friends. We are tempted to let others think we are something that we are not. We are tempted to tell parents or teachers only part of the truth. We are tempted to let others take the blame for what we have done.

So often, however, our temptations come in the form of an invitation or a dare to do something "just for kicks" or "just this once." We know pretty well that it's something we have no business doing, but we give in. The "just this once" becomes "one more time" until one day we realize that we are stuck for life with a bad habit, a secret sin, or the difficulties they got us into. Or we may realize that we have taken on a certain vocabulary, or developed certain mannerisms that we are not proud of. The little white lie has grown into an ugly black one, and we can't shake it. That tiny insincerity in congratulating a friend has developed into a disgusting "drippiness" that everyone notices. That just-this-once going with the crowd when we knew better has us in hot water up to here.

Learning how to handle temptation isn't easy. It's a lifetime task. You no sooner work your way around one temptation than you are faced by another. So what do you do? We all have to find our own answers, but here are some suggestions that may help:

1. First of all, you can learn to identify temptation as temptation. Don't fool yourself.

2. Then you can face up to it honestly. You can ask such questions as, What will be the results if I do this thing just this once? Is this something that squares with what I believe is right? Will what I do hurt other people —friends, parents, those who love and trust me?

3. You can go to persons who can help you think through your problems—parents, teachers, ministers.

4. You can pray for wisdom to recognize temptation for what it is and for strength to stand firm when you have reached a decision.

5. You can turn to your Bible for assurance:

No temptation has overtaken you that is not common to man. God is faithful, and he will not let you be tempted beyond your strength, but with the temptation will also provide the way of escape, that you may be able to endure it. (I Cor. 10:13)

O God, pull me up sharply when I am about to give in to temptation. Strengthen me to do the things that I believe are right for me. I pray in the name of Jesus whose example I am trying to follow. Amen.

What Does God Expect?

WHAT DOES GOD EXPECT OF YOU?

There are a couple of things he *doesn't* expect.

God doesn't expect you just to accept a set of beliefs that somebody will hand you. Not that beliefs aren't important. They're terribly important, for what we believe determines the way we act. We can't escape the tough job of reasoning out what it means to be a Christian. But —you could figure that out, and still not be doing what God expects you to do.

God doesn't expect you to be perfect. He made you a human being, and he made you free. You can do what you pretty well please, and if you are like all the rest of the human race, you sometimes please to be bad. And sometimes when you are trying to be good, you make mistakes. God knows you're like that. No doubt he wishes you weren't (and he will help you be *less* like that), but he knows who you are and how you are, and he knows that's not perfect. Besides, you could be perfect (always following the rules) and you still would not be doing what God expects of you.

Then what does he expect?

He expects you to accept and love him.

That's all. But that's a lot.

Christians use the word faith to describe their relationship to God, this relationship of acceptance and love. To have faith in God—*to live in faith*—what does that mean?

It means knowing—really believing—that God has made this world, that he runs it.

It means being sure—really sure—that God loves us so fully that we can trust our lives to him, no matter what.

It means being faithful to him—loyal, that is, to what he calls us to do—out of thankfulness for his love.

So we know these three things when we have faith:

1. *This is God's world.*
2. *God loves me, so I can trust him.*
3. *Out of gratitude, I will live as he wants me to.*

". . . live as he wants me to." There's the trouble, all right. And that is what we spend our lives doing: trying to find out, with his help, what he wants us to do.

If you really love me, you will keep the commandments I have given you and I shall ask the Father to give you someone else to stand by you, to be with you always. I mean the Spirit of Truth, whom the world cannot accept, for it can neither see nor recognize that Spirit. But you recognize him, for he is with you now and will be in your hearts. (JOHN 14:15-17 Phillips)

O God, in whose love and care I have come into this world, and by whose love I live, help me to show my love for you by finding your will for my life, and doing it. Let thy Spirit lead me, so that I can follow. Encourage me so that I shall have strength. Accept my thanks, so that my service can be done in gratitude to you for your love, and for no other reason. AMEN.

accomplish big things by . . .

Tending to Trifles

THE STORY GOES THAT SOME FRIENDS OF THE GREAT sculptor Michelangelo visited him one day when he was working on a statue. About a month later they came back again and found him still working away on the same statue. One of them asked him what he had been doing all that time. The great artist pointed out that he had smoothed a line here, done a little polishing there, taken off a few flakes of marble in another spot.

"But these are only trifles . . ." his friends said.

"True, they are trifles," Michelangelo said, "but trifles make perfection, and perfection is no trifle."

How do you feel about trifles, about details? Most of us can think of many instances where attention to trifles would have made a world of difference. Many a theme that drew only a grade of C would have rated a B, or even an A, if the writer had taken care of trifles —a comma here, a capital there, handwriting that could be read, or a neat paper. Many a test tube and beaker in the science lab would still be whole if the experimenter had paid more attention to trifles. Many a student would have cinched that summer job if his appearance hadn't said only too clearly that he was not interested in trifles.

True, we cannot all become Michelangelos. But we can prepare ourselves to make the most of our talents and abilities by applying one of the secrets of his success, this careful attention to detail. To others this may seem only trifling; to us it may mean the difference between success and failure.

The apostle Paul must have had something of this in mind when he advised young Timothy:

Do your best to present yourself to God as one approved, a workman who has no need to be ashamed, rightly handling the word of truth. (II Tim. 2:15)

Father, help me take time for the little things, for the trifles, today and every day. In doing the small things well I would learn how to do the larger things more perfectly. Show me how to do this so that I may bring every part of my life into harmony with your will for me. Amen.

no matter how far you go . . .

You Can't Run Away From God

LOTS OF MEN HAVE TRIED TO RUN AWAY FROM GOD. Jonah didn't like it when God told him to go to the city of Nineveh and tell about the justice of God. So he bought passage on a ship, and tried to run away to Tarshish, where he hoped God could not find him. But God hurled a great wind on the sea, and Jonah really had troubles. He couldn't get away. Nobody can run that far.

Elijah, God's prophet, tried the same trick. Once when the king destroyed some of Elijah's priests, the prophet became angry and pulled out for the mountains. He sat through tornado and lightning and storm—but finally God, in a still, small voice spoke to Elijah. He found he couldn't run away. Nobody can, because nobody can run that far.

In England there was a young man who tried to run away. Francis Thompson ran until he couldn't run anymore. A friend found him almost dead from drunkenness in a London gutter and brought him home. Finally Francis Thompson let God speak to him, and he became a great poet. His most famous poem, "The Hound of Heaven," pictures God as a hound who pursues men all their days until at last he catches them. Francis Thompson should know. He tried, and found that nobody can run away—not for long. Nobody can run that far.

Sometimes we, too, try to run away from God. We look at the world we live in and see unhappiness and greed and selfishness. Then we take a good look at ourselves and see much that is not good—we often think first of ourselves, forgetting the people around us who do not have the advantages we have. So, when we look around us, there is not much that is pleasant—and we wish we didn't have to bother with so much misery.

But God is calling to us every day when he helps us to see the troubles in ourselves and in our world. In our hearts he plants a response to the world's need, and we know that we ought to help.

And then what do we do? Run away?

Sometimes we do. But we can't. Nobody can run that far. God's love pursues us, and will overtake us and help us learn to live the kind of lives he wants us to live. In the end, we must let God have his way with us.

Because we do run away sometimes, we can pray this prayer from the Bible:

Whither shall I go from thy Spirit?
Or whither shall I flee from thy presence?
If I ascend to heaven, thou art there!
If I make my bed in Sheol, thou art there!
If I take the wings of the morning
and dwell in the uttermost parts of the sea
even there thy hand shall lead me,
and thy right hand shall hold me.
If I say, "Let only darkness cover me,
and the light about me be night,"

even the darkness is not dark to thee,
the night is bright as the day;
for darkness is as light with thee.
For thou didst form my inward parts,
thou didst knit me together in my mother's womb.
I praise thee, for thou art fearful and wonderful.
(Ps. 139:7-14)

In Jesus' name. AMEN.

so you have . . .

A Handicap

EVER FEEL SORRY FOR YOURSELF? EVER TALK TO YOURself something like this: "Sure, I could be an athlete too if I didn't have this handicap. He never had polio, or cerebral palsy, or any of those diseases that leave a person crippled. Or, he was never in a car wreck that left him with a twisted back, or minus an arm or leg. . . . Or, he never had to walk on crutches, or get around in a wheel chair, or wear braces, or . . ."

Whenever we begin making excuses to ourselves like this it's a signal for time out—time out to do some good hard thinking.

First of all, remember that nearly every person has

a handicap. You're not alone in that respect. Maybe the handicap doesn't show—like the weak heart from rheumatic fever, or the eyes that can't spot a friend across the street, or the trick knee that may throw you any minute. We all have our imperfections physically or mentally or emotionally.

It's a good thing to remember too that what other people consider a handicap doesn't necessarily have to be a handicap to you. Maybe you can't be the athlete of the year. Maybe there are lots of things you won't ever be able to do. But you can make the most of the abilities you have.

Plenty of people who are numbered among the all-time greats in their fields have had terrific handicaps. The glorious music of Beethoven is the work of a deaf composer. The great actress Sarah Bernhardt continued her career in spite of the loss of a leg. A diabetic from the age of nine, Billy Talbert became a national and international tennis champion. Much of James Thurber's writing was done with an oversized black crayon while he was losing his eyesight.

As we think of the accomplishments of these and others that we know, two things become very clear: first, these people did not give in to feeling sorry for themselves; and second, they made the best use of whatever talent or ability they had. In so doing they were able to go around the handicap, to achieve in spite of it.

Maybe yours is not a major handicap. But whether it's large or small, what are you doing about it? Feeling sorry for yourself won't help. Depending on others won't help. This is a personal matter that must be faced by you alone, squarely and courageously. But in doing so, we need to remember that we can find help. Jesus, doing the work of his Father, spent the greater part his ministry in helping those who had handicaps of one sort or another. In his life and teachings we can find the help to go around our own handicaps, to make the most of the abilities we have.

Men have different gifts, but it is the same Spirit who gives them. There are different ways of serving God, but it is the same Lord who is served. God works through different men in different ways, but it is the same God who achieves his purposes through them all. Each man is given his gift by the Spirit that he may make the most of it. (I Cor. 12:2-8 Phillips)

O God, it is so easy to give in to our handicaps. Forgive us when we do this. Show us how we may develop the talents and abilities we have and thus find a way around these handicaps. Keep us alert to new ideas, ready to try new things, grateful to those who give of their time and efforts to help us. In Jesus' name we pray. Amen *when you wonder . . .*

What Is God Like?

IF YOU WERE GOD, HOW WOULD YOU LET THE WORLD know what you are like?

God tried several ways.

He thought maybe men could look at the lives of other men and get some idea of what God is like. After all, he had made man in his own image.

Then God said, Let us make man in our own image. (GEN. 1:26).

But that didn't work. Man made a mess of things, as you remember, and it was hard to tell that man was ever made in God's image.

So God decided he would call the Hebrews to be his people. Through their leaders, he could tell them how good men live, and they could be servants to all the rest of the world, telling them about God's way.

But that didn't work either. Even though God led the people out of their troubles into Egypt and gave them a homeland and laws for living, they were not true to him, and they didn't tell the world what God was like.

And then it happened. God sent a messenger into the world so that men could see what he was like. Funny thing, though. His messenger didn't come as a king or an emperor, or even an angel.

He was born a baby, in a cow's stall. And he grew up,

just like other babies grow up. And finally he began his work, going about the countryside of Palestine telling people about God's world, and about his love, and about what God wanted them to do. Everywhere he went, people were glad to hear him.

Some people believed what he said, and they became his workers, helping him visit the people around and about. But lots of people thought it was wicked of a man to say the things he said, and to claim to speak God's truth. So they killed him. They nailed him to a cross, and buried him in a tomb, and washed their hands of the whole affair.

But that didn't work. This man who was walking around Palestine, and whom they had killed, was God's Son.

The next thing anybody knew, Christ the Son was back out in the world, encouraging his workers, still meeting men who wanted him, still telling men what God is like. And to this day, he walks the ways of earth. Someone points him out to us and we say, "That's it. Now we know. God is like that. That is God; that is God's Son."

And when we let him, he comes into our lives so fully that we come to know what it means to be alive in this world. He saves us from the little, dragging days that we might have lived, and fills us with truth and goodness, and reminds us that nothing can keep God from loving us. And we are filled with new strength and see with new vision.

In all things we are more than conquerors through him who loved us. For I am sure that neither death, nor life, nor angels, nor principalities, nor things present, nor things to come, nor powers, nor height, nor depth, nor anything else in all creation, will be able to separate us from the love of God in Christ Jesus our Lord.

(Rom. 8:37-39)

For thy unending love, O God, I thank thee. Help me to accept thy love and let it lead me in the way I should go—serving others, expressing my thankfulness. Amen.

nobody likes . . .

A Show-Off

We get pretty disgusted with the fellow who goes around bragging all the time—about what he has, where he has been, what he can do. We get pretty disgusted with the girl who makes a point of overdressing, who lets everybody know how much money her family has, who always grabs the center of attention. Maybe John is a champion athlete, or best voice in the chorus. Maybe Mary is an honor student or winner of the drama trophy. But we can't stand to hear them brag about it.

It's pretty easy to become a show-off. We are trying so hard to impress our friends, our parents, or other adults. We want so much for them to think well of us, to like us. We feel that just being ourselves isn't quite enough—we must let them know all about our good points, our achievements, our talents and abilities. So we start bragging. We start showing off. We try to let them see us as the person we would like to have them know. Justifiable pride has given way to boasting and, without really realizing what we have been doing, we ourselves have become show-offs. We have actually insulted the intelligence of our friends by expecting them to be taken in by our show-offishness!

The apostle Paul was firmly convinced that if we make love the center of our lives we can overcome our personal difficulties as well as our difficulties with one another. If we have a basic respect for others, that is, if we love them as God loves us, then we do not try to take them in with bragging and with showing off.

For by the grace given to me I bid every one among you not to think of himself more highly than he ought to think. . . . Make love your aim, and earnestly desire the spiritual gifts. (ROM. 12:3; I COR. 14:1)

O God, help me to grow up in my thinking and behavior so that I will not allow myself to become a show-off. Help me, too, to be loving and understanding with others when they are showing off. I want to make love my "aim." Show me how. AMEN.

when you're wondering . . .

What Friends Expect of Friends

"FUNNY THING, MOM. YESTERDAY I DIDN'T EVEN KNOW Ted—but today I helped him find his softball and now we're friends!"

All of us like to have friends—many friends who like us and who want to be with us, who help us out and who let us know when we can help them.

Sometimes, though, we get mixed up about friends and what they expect of each other.

Are friends those who are always doing things for us or giving us things?

Many seek the favor of a generous man,
and everyone is a friend to a man who gives gifts.
(PROV. 19:6)

But this is not *true* friendship, is it?

Are friends those who always agree with us and help us get our way? This can hardly be right—sometimes we want the wrong things, and a true friend would not agree with us in wanting what is not good.

Well, then, what is a friend? Isn't he *a person who tries to understand and to help?* If he does these two things, we think he is truly a friend, don't we? And if we are trying to *be* a friend, then it is our job to understand the people around us and to go out of our way to help them in any way we can.

This means that we learn to be patient, so that when our friends are angry, we try to wait for their anger to pass away, rather than become angry at them in turn. When they have a problem, we try to listen to them and help them think it through. Or we may show our friendship in simpler ways, like helping find Ted's softball.

Do you remember the story of David and Saul—how their friendship became cold, and King Saul tried to destroy David? David fled into the wilderness to save his life. But Saul called out his army and tried to find him. Once King Saul entered a dark cave, not knowing David was hiding in it. David quietly cut a piece of Saul's robe and let him escape, to let the king know that he could have killed him but did not. David was patient and loyal, even when his friend had turned away from him.

When you begin the process of trying to understand and help those around you, you discover—often unexpectedly—that you are making friends without even trying. Once you know what it is friends expect of each other, friendship is not such a big problem. You just begin going about the business of getting to know others better and helping them out whenever you can.

Today think a while about some of the new people you have met. Would you like for them to become your friends?

Have you tried to be understanding and helpful to them?

Think about this statement from Proverbs (18:24):

There are friends who pretend to be friends, but there is a friend who sticks closer than a brother.

Pray that God will show you ways to be the kind of person who understands and helps those around him. Thank God for the friends he gives you when you are helpful and understanding. And thank him for the friends he gives you who stick with you when you are hard to get along with.

are you really . . .

Too Busy?

"I'D LIKE TO DO IT BUT I JUST DON'T HAVE TIME." EVER use that excuse? There are so many interests that call to us, so many books to be read, so many records to listen to, so many friends, so many studies, so many church activities. We find ourselves going in circles, always in a hurry, always making excuses.

Is it really true when we say we don't have enough time? Each of us has as much time as his neighbor does —twenty-four hours in every day. But what we get done in those twenty-four hours is another matter. Often the person who talks the loudest about not having enough time is the one who makes the poorest use of it. On the other hand, people who seem to accomplish the most waste no time in telling you how busy they are. If you watch these people closely you usually discover several secrets about how they use their time.

1. They spend their time doing the things that are important to them. After all, why give up an hour here or an afternoon there doing something that you're really not interested in?

2. They give top priority to the things that need doing immediately. If a history test is coming up, it's rather silly to spend all your study time on science, isn't it?

3. They look ahead and plan their time. True, there are always emergencies and the best-laid plan may have to be scrapped. But having some idea in the morning as to how they will use their time that day helps keep tasks in order and cuts down on confusion.

4. They have learned to plug up the time leaks. If it only takes twenty minutes to wash the dishes, why spend an extra ten minutes trying to get out of doing them? Why waste time being too early or too late for classes, or dates, or whatever you're doing?

5. They seldom "kill time." They make the minutes count, for they have learned that once time is gone it is gone forever. We can never make up time—only what we should have done in that time.

Of all the gifts that come from God, time is one of the most precious. We are free to use it as we will. How we use the twenty-four hours given to us each day determines not only what we accomplish but what we become as persons.

Today think about how you are using time. Are you allowing others to waste it for you? Are you making good use of the minutes between large tasks? Are you planning so that you can make the best use of each day?

If any of you lacks wisdom, let him ask God who gives to all men generously and without reproaching, and it will be given him. . . . Every good endowment and every perfect gift is from above, coming down from the Father of lights with whom there is no variation or shadow due to change. (JAMES 1:5, 17)

O God, I give thanks for the wonderful gift of time. Guide me as I try to learn how to make the best use of this gift, how to use it each day to do the things you want me to do. AMEN.

you stop and think . . .

When Someone Dies

AS EACH YEAR COMES AND GOES, WE WONDER A LITTLE bit more about that strange experience that every person knows he must face: death.

Even when we are young, death begins to haunt us with its threat. We know members of our family and sometimes close friends who come face to face with death. Some live through these times. But others die. And we begin to wonder what death is all about.

Job wondered. And the more he wondered the angrier he got. To him, it was wicked of God to create man, give him life and happiness, children and land, and then allow him to be destroyed.

For there is hope for a tree,
if it be cut down, that it will sprout again,
and that its shoots will not cease.
Though its root grow old in the earth,
and its stump die in the ground,
yet at the scent of water it will bud
and put forth branches like a young plant.
But man dies, and is laid low;
man breathes his last, and where is he?
As waters fail from a lake,
and a river wastes away and dries up,
So man lies down and rises not again;
till the heavens are no more he will not awake,
or be roused out of his sleep. . . .
If a man die, shall he live again?

(Job 14:7-12, 14)

This question that has always disturbed men was answered with great joy on the first Easter.

For Jesus, the Christ, though tortured and killed by

his enemies, was not defeated by death. God raised him from his tomb into the world again where he entered the hearts of those who loved and accepted him. And by his conquest of death, his followers believe that they too will live again after their bodies die and are seen no more on earth.

For those who know Christ, this grand hope is cause for rejoicing, for it gives a clear and strong answer to Job's question. Christ has met and defeated death, and has thus given his followers hope that they, too, shall live.

Today, while you are quietly thinking about death, and about God's gift of eternal life, let God's Spirit speak to you.

Thank God for life that has no end . . . for life that ***is*** *full of his love, from the very beginning of our lives . . . and always. . . .*

when you question . . .

A Friend's Sincerity

DO YOU REMEMBER THE FABLE ABOUT THE FOX AND THE cat? The fox wanted to get some chestnuts out of the fire but he knew he would burn himself in doing it. So he began telling the cat how smart and how quick she was. The cat, flattered by his compliments, reached into the fire and pulled out the chestnuts. She also pulled out a badly burned paw. And, what was worse, the fox made fun of her for being so foolish.

A fable, as you know, is a story that tells a great truth. It isn't hard to see the truth in this one! How often we are like the fox. We want someone to help us get our chestnuts out of the fire—lend us a notebook so we won't flunk a test, do the hard work we're responsible for in having a party, ask favors that we should ask for ourselves. We try to take advantage of our friends—get them to do the unpleasant things for us. Like the fox, we think that "flattery will get you everywhere."

Sometimes though we're more like the cat. We are so eager for another's approval that we listen to what we know is flattery. We allow ourselves to be talked into doing all sorts of foolish things. And when we do we usually end up like the cat—we are hurt and discouraged.

Men and women of true Christian character have learned that they must take responsibility for their own actions, that they cannot expect others to get their chestnuts out of the fire for them. They have learned, too, that flattery, whether given or accepted, is a form of insincerity and they know that insincerity is not in keeping with their desire to become followers of Jesus.

Like the glaze covering an earthen vessel are smooth lips with an evil heart . . . and a flattering mouth works ruin. (Prov. 26:23, 28*b*)

O God, keep me from taking advantage of other persons, from getting them to do the things I should do for myself. Keep me from using flattery in dealing with my friends and strengthen me to turn a deaf ear when others flatter me. I pray in the name of Jesus whose life was one of sincerity in all he said and did. AMEN.

you can't always tell . . .

When the Price Is Right

SEVERAL FELLOWS ONCE WENT INTO THE DEPARTMENT store where their teacher worked on Saturdays and decided to mix him up. They switched price tags around a bit. Next morning when a customer asked the price of chocolate fudge, the clerk looked at a tag that read fifteen cents per yard! Refrigerators were a bargain at forty-nine cents a pound. And ladies' hats were marked "$275 installed."

The things around us often have the wrong price tag on them too, because we sometimes put the wrong values on our experience. Some of the things that are best for us we think are useless; and we put a big price on some things that are really worthless. We may think vacations and chocolate fudge and new books are very meaningful, and put a high value on them. Other things may not seem worth too much to us—raking the yard, for instance, or getting lessons.

This business of finding out how to put the right value on every part of our lives is one of our major tasks as we grow up. Our happiness depends on finding the right way to rate every part of our experience.

Jesus' disciples had this same problem. Here is what he told them:

Don't worry about living—wondering what you are going to eat or drink, or what you are going to wear. Surely life is more important than food, and the body is more important than the clothes you wear. Look at the birds in the sky. They never sow nor reap nor store away in barns, and yet your Heavenly Father feeds them. Aren't you much more valuable to him than they are? . . .

So don't worry and don't keep saying, 'What shall we eat, what shall we drink or what shall we wear?' That is what pagans are always looking for; your Heavenly Father knows that you need them all. Set your heart on his kingdom and his goodness, and all these things will come to you as a matter of course.

(MATT. 6:25-26, 31-33 Phillips)

How can one learn to value life properly?

First of all, you need to decide what the most important things in life are. Think about them now. *What are they?*

Next, you must decide if you are willing to seek these really valuable things above everything else. *Are you?*

Then, you must offer yourself to God, determined to seek the things he has led you to value so highly. *Will you?*

Now . . . *have you?*

Our Father, as I live my life day by day help me make right choices, learning as each day passes what things are worth giving myself to. Strengthen me as I try to follow the high ideals I have accepted. In Jesus' name.
AMEN

everybody wants to have . . .

A Good Name

A WELL-KNOWN PERSON IS OFTEN NAMED AS THE HEAD of a civic movement, a charity organization, or a fund-raising campaign. His name appears in all the publicity, he poses for pictures for the press and television, and his name heads the list on letterheads. He has been selected because he is respected by others for what he is and what he has done. His name counts for something.

Each of us, too, can make his name count for something. And the teens are the years when we begin. What does your name count for—a grouch, a character, a mouse, a quitter? Or does your name count for a clear thinker; a person who is honest, friendly, and dependable; one who will stay with a job until it's finished; one who will give another a fair deal?

There is a story told about a boy who just could not seem to get into any of the school activities. This made him so unhappy that he continually went about with a long face. When yearbook elections came up he was voted the school's worst grouch. At last he counted for something! But in order to make his name continue to count for something he had to continue being a grouch!

Making a name count for something good calls for some special effort on our part. We dare not drift along and allow ourselves to be drawn into doing the things that are not in keeping with our standards of right and wrong. We have to keep trying over and over again to live at our best every hour of every day.

Think about your name today. What are you doing to make it a good name? Could you do more?

A good name is to be chosen rather than great riches, and favor is better than silver or gold. . . . Blessed is the man who makes the Lord his trust.

(Prov. 22:1, Ps. 40:4*a*)

It is not always easy to make our names count for the good things, Father. But I know that you can help me, that you can show me the way to make mine a good name. Forgive me for mistakes I have made in doing this, and guide and strengthen me as I try to become a person whose name counts for good things. AMEN.

for those days when you say . . .

But I Don't *Like* to Study!

A FELLOW I KNOW IS ALWAYS SAYING, "WELL, IF WE had any ham we could have ham and eggs—if we had any eggs."

It is all these *if's* that keep us from having lots of things we want. You can't have ham and eggs, can you, *if* you don't have any ham or any eggs?

It's good to remember how important the if's are when we find it tough to get down to the business of studying. When we get into that mood we wish more than anything else that we would never again have to look inside a book, or open a classroom door!

But then is just the time to remember that some of the things we do very much want depend on our getting down the books and getting to work. Just think now about the days ahead, and what you want to get from them, and what you want to offer to them.

You want to become a mature adult . . .
fully aware of the world around you,
unafraid of the threats around you,
anxious to serve the people around you.
You want even now to fulfill your own role in life . . .
finding what it means to be yourself,
learning what it means to give yourself,
seeking goals to challenge yourself.
You want to plan with care . . .
the work that you will give your life to,
the home that you will establish,
the ideals that you will keep and honor always.

Now, all of these things (as well as others you have thought of) depend in a large degree on what you do with your school days. *If* you want to fulfill your hopes for the future, you'll have to take today's tough jobs seriously. The dreams you dream now will follow you always; and the hard work you do now will prepare you for the rest of your days.

So, even when studying is just plain hard—when all the fun is gone out of it (and thank goodness, there are plenty of days when studying *is* fun!)—for the sake of many wonderful things you want to realize a little further down your days, stick to it.

Do not be deceived; God is not mocked, for whatever a man sows, that he will also reap. . . . And let us not

grow weary in well-doing, for in due season we shall reap, if we do not lose heart. (GAL. 6:7, 9)

Today, as you pray, ask God to bless your plans for the days ahead, and to encourage you to keep on studying, even when the going is hard.

when you are . . .

Learning to Pray

THE SKILL OF THE JUGGLER IS ALWAYS FASCINATING. He can keep two or three balls bouncing with his head while he spins plates on his fingers and twirls hoops on his ankles. He can switch from one position to another instantly and set up an entirely different routine. We watch in amazement. How does he do it?

The answer of course is practice and concentration. Each movement has been practiced over and over again. His timing has been worked out to the split second. Hours and hours have gone into perfecting each small part of his act. Then the parts have been carefully fitted together and there has been more practice. By the time the act is finally ready, movements have become almost automatic. But not for one instant while he is performing does the juggler dare to let his mind wander, or forget what he is doing. A good performance demands that he be alert every moment.

The same rules hold for many skills that we try to learn. Take learning to pray, for example. We learn only by doing. At first our prayers may be very simple ones and we may find ourselves having trouble talking with God. But as we try again and again, we discover that we are learning.

It may be easy—almost a reflex—to turn our minds to God in thankfulness when we see a beautiful sunset, or when some special opportunity comes to us, or when for a moment we catch a glimpse of his goodness in the lives of people. But there are other types of prayer that we must work at continually. We must learn how to take our problems to God and how to let him help us solve them. We must learn how to help others through our prayers. We must learn how to say "I'm sorry" and ask God's forgiveness. And we must learn how to put aside our own desires, our own needs, our own ideas of what is right and ask God to take us and use us for his purposes.

Often a time of prayer dissolves into nothingness because we do not keep our minds fixed on our purpose and on God. Learning how to pray also means learning how to concentrate, how to control our minds and feelings. For most of us this is a lifetime task. But each day's practice helps us learn. And each prayer opens up new ways to know and to love God. We learn to pray by praying.

Ask, and it will be given you; seek, and you will find; knock, and it will be opened to you. For every one who asks receives, and he who seeks finds, and to him who knocks it will be opened. (MATT. 7:7-8)

O God, teach me to pray. Help me practice daily. Show me how to keep my mind from straying to other things and how to keep my selfishness from intruding when I pray. This I ask in the name of Jesus whose teachings help me learn about prayer. AMEN.

in your crowd . . .

Do You Set the Temperature?

TWO LITTLE INSTRUMENTS. THEY LOOK A LOT ALIKE.

One is a thermometer.

The other's a thermostat.

But there is a whale of a difference in the two. The thermometer tells you how hot your room is. The thermostat lets you decide how hot you want it.

What are you—a thermometer, or a thermostat?

When you're with your friends, and the evening is really rolling along, and suddenly somebody suggests something you aren't quite sure you like, what do *you* do? At school, when some of your friends are taking the easy way out by cheating—"just a little bit"—what do *you* do? When someone new and a little bit "different" moves into your neighborhood and the crowd is rather cool to him, what do *you* do?

Well, if you're a thermometer, you just record the temperature of your surroundings. You go right along with the crowd on their spree, even when you feel deep down that you shouldn't. You cheat "just a little bit" too. And you turn a cold shoulder to the lonesome new neighbor around the corner. You just reflect what everyone else is doing. You're a thermometer.

But you *might* be a thermostat. You might help set the temperature in your gang. Ready for a spree? "Not this thermostat. I know what I think is right, and what I think is wrong. Count me out!" Cheat? "Not this thermostat. I'm having something to say about how I live my life. Let me set the temperature around here, if you please." Stranger in the block? "Show him to me. I don't have to go along with this childish snub. Not this thermostat!"

Anyone can help determine what the tone of his group will be, if he can accept the responsibility that is his. You can certainly decide what *you* will do. And by making good choices and maintaining your friendships at the same time you can begin to change the temperature of the whole crowd. Try it.

With eyes wide open to the mercies of God, I beg you, my brothers, as an act of intelligent worship, to give him

your bodies, as a living sacrifice, consecrated to him and acceptable by him. Don't let the world around you squeeze you into its own mold, but let God remold your minds from within, so that you may prove in practice that the plan of God for you is good, meets all his demands and moves toward the goal of true maturity.

(Rom. 12:1-2 Phillips)

Help me to know, O God, that you have called me to be true to you in every group I belong to. Help me to set the pace, speaking what I know is true, and living according to what I know is right. In Jesus' name I pray.

Amen

take another look at . . .

The Ordinary Things

Here is a short list of things:

toothpaste
soap
hot water
toast
ball-point pen
telephone
notebook paper

Just ordinary things, you say. And you are right. They are just ordinary things—things we use every day of our lives without giving them even a passing thought.

But what a change there would be if even one of these things should be suddenly removed from our lives! How terrible to have to go to school, or church, or on a date without benefit of toothpaste, hot water, or soap! Perhaps there are moments when we almost wish there were no such things as ball-point pens and notebook paper, but how could teen-agers exist without telephones?

We have grown so used to these ordinary, everyday things that we take them pretty much for granted. We probably never stop to think of all that goes into the production of the toothpaste we use each morning—the work of laboratory technicians in developing just the right combination of ingredients, the labor involved in actually producing the product, the planning and effort and the many workers involved in packaging, advertising, and selling it. When we do pause to consider the ordinary everyday things that make us healthier, happier, and more comfortable, and that make our tasks easier, there comes a deepened sense of appreciation. We begin to realize what a wonderful world we live in! We begin to see that it is a world full of God's wonders—not only the great natural wonders, but the wonders of ordinary, everyday things that he has given men and women the knowledge to create.

Why not spend some time today thinking about the everyday things that you so often take for granted. As you list them in your mind, or on a sheet of paper, thank God for each one.

> **Praise the Lord.**
> **I will give thanks to the Lord with my whole heart . . .**
> **Great are the works of the Lord,**
> **studied by all who have pleasure in them.**
> **Full of honor and majesty is his work,**
> **and his righteousness endures for ever.**
> **(Ps. 111:1-3)**

O God, I give thanks today for all your wonderful gifts. But I am especially thankful today for the ordinary everyday things that add so much to my life. I will try not to take these so much for granted in the future but will always try to remember that they are your good gifts and give thanks for them. AMEN.

take a look at yourself . . .

On Your Birthday

WHAT ARE YOU WORTH? WELL—MELTED DOWN AND packaged in the right way, you're worth just a little over a dollar! You are made up of just about enough sugar to sweeten a glass of tea, enough fat to make seven bars of soap, enough salt to sprinkle on a fried egg, enough iron to make a small nail, enough sulphur to chase your dog's fleas away, and enough lime to whitewash a tree house!

But is that *you?*

Are you just a package of chemicals put together in a marvelous way? Or is there more to you than that?

Your birthday might be a good time to do a little thinking about just what you are. One thing is sure. The people who love you and care for you don't think you're a combination of chemicals shaped into a person. They know there is more to you than that. They know you love them, for instance, and love can't be explained in terms of iron or sulphur or fat, can it? They know that once in a while, you get a glimpse of what life is all about. And you can't explain *that* as a chemical reaction, now can you?

No—there is more to *you* than can be measured on any chemist's scale. This is what the Bible says about the kind of man God made:

In the day that the Lord God made the earth and the heavens, when no plant of the field was yet in the earth and no herb of the field had yet sprung up . . . the Lord God formed man of dust from the ground, and breathed into his nostrils the breath of life; and man became a living being. And the Lord God planted

a garden in Eden, in the east; and there he put the man whom he had formed. (GEN. 2:4-5, 7-8)

According to the Bible, you see, man was formed from God's very breath.

God's Spirit makes us what we are, and this makes all the difference in our lives. It means that we belong to God. All that we have and are—including the gift of our very lives—comes as a gift from God.

Unfortunately—and *here* is a serious thought for your birthday—we, like the first man, do not always remember who we are. We forget that we belong to God, and sometimes live as if we were our own masters. When we do—when we deny that God's spirit lives in us and makes us who we are—then we are just so much sugar and salt and lime!

On this special day, when you are thinking about yourself, about who you are, and who God intends for you to be, make this your prayer:

O God, help me remember on this special day that you have made me. Since I am yours, teach me how to do the things you would like for me to do. Help me find out what kind of person I should become. And help me to live my life—the life you have given me—happily and unselfishly, so that those I am with will know that I belong to you. In Jesus' name I pray. AMEN.

it's never too late for ...

Righting a Wrong

THE PEOPLE OF MASSACHUSETTS HAVE OFFICIALLY righted a wrong committed in their state many years ago. You have read about the crime. It is a sad tale that begins with the false accusations brought against innocent persons by two teen-age girls. What began as something of a prank resulted in the hanging of twenty-two innocent persons as "witches."

When the witchcraft hysteria began to die down and honest people began to think through what had been happening they realized the horror of their actions. All of this occurred in 1692. Within twenty years all but six of the so-called witches had been cleared of the charges against them. These six persons had no relatives to clear their names. But the conscience of the good people of Massachusetts could not rest and they kept working. On August 28, 1957, the governor signed a special bill by which the six were finally cleared.

It took a long time to right the great wrong that resulted from those first false accusations—two hundred and sixty-five years, to be exact. But something was finally done about it. Perhaps this bit of history says something to us.

To be sure, we don't go around today accusing people of being witches. Yet, how often and how glibly we sometimes brand another person as dishonest. When a classmate makes an A on a quiz, it's easy to say, "Oh, I could have made an A too if I did what he did." The tone of voice and attitude says clearly that he cheated. It's a simple matter to cover up jealousy and plant suspicion in others' minds with remarks such as, "I could wear good clothes too if my father made his money like John's father does." And how easy to accuse another of all sorts of things merely by referring to him as an "outsider" or as being "different." What we suggest can often do more harm than accusing a person of a specific act. But having so falsely accused another we can do something about it. We can right the wrong if we really want to do so.

Think about all this today. Does it have any application in your life? Have you wronged others by what you have said or by the way you have said it? What are you going to do about righting any such wrongs?

Judge not, and you will not be judged; condemn not, and you will not be condemned; forgive, and you will be forgiven; give, and it will be given to you.

(Luke 6:37-38*a*)

Forgive me when I accuse others falsely, Father. Strengthen me to right whatever wrongs I have committed and show me how to guard my thoughts and actions so that these wrongs may not be repeated. Amen.

Where Am I Going?

Do you know where you're going?

Lots of people don't—they're like that man who jumped on his horse and rode off in all directions.

But a lot of people do know where they're going. And you would like to know also. It's no fun to be unsure of yourself, not quite certain about what direction your life is taking. You wish somebody would come along and straighten you out.

Of course, you are the only person who can do that. Nobody else, no matter how smart he is and no matter how much he loves you, can set the direction of your life, and get you on the way.

But you can.

You can decide now, in these days of important decisions—where you'd like to go. Where do you want your life to take you? What goals will you choose and keep before you all your life? Where can you serve as no one else can? These are questions you are often thinking about. At some point along your way, you must make up your mind and choose the goals you want. A great dream out in front will pull you toward your goals like nothing else can. But you must also commit yourself to the task of making your dreams come true.

You can work like everything to reach that goal. You know people who know where they would like to go, but who don't work at it. There's the boy who wants to go to college, but who doesn't plan to do a thing to help himself get there. And there's the girl who wants to go to camp—but doesn't lift a hand to make her dream come true. If you want to go somewhere, you have to work at it, not just wish.

You can keep yourself open to God's leading. Sometimes the dreams we dream turn out not to be the dreams God has for us. You might want to be a pilot, or a writer. But your plans may not fit into God's bigger plan for you—so you need to live closely enough to him to know what he wants you to do.

And as God leads, you can follow. When you say No to God—even once—you make it more difficult to hear his voice the next time he speaks. When you hear him, answer. When he points the way, thank him, and walk in it.

And remember—God expects you to keep moving toward the high goals you have set. Get to work!

Yet, my brothers, I do not consider myself to have "arrived," spiritually, nor do I consider myself already perfect. But I keep going on, grasping ever more firmly that purpose for which Christ grasped me. My brothers, I do not consider myself to have fully grasped it even now. But I do concentrate on this: I leave the past behind and with hands outstretched to whatever lies ahead I go straight for the goal—my reward the honor of being called by God in Christ. All of us who are spiritually

adult should set ourselves this sort of ambition, and if at present you cannot see this, yet you will find that this is the attitude which God is leading you to adopt. It is important that we go forward in the light of such truth as we have ourselves attained to.

(PHIL. 3:13-16 Phillips)

O God, who hast set before me so many choices and so many possible goals, lead me as I take my choices. Help me choose high goals. And do not let me be satisfied with just choosing the right goals, but show me ways to reach those goals with thy help. I pray in Jesus' name. AMEN.

you can share in the ...

Beauty Around You

MANY TEEN-AGERS ARE COLLECTORS. SOME COLLECT rocks, or butterflies, or Indian relics, or stamps. Others make valuable collections of coins or foreign dolls. And many have made quite a collection of records and photographs of their favorite entertainers. Each of these collections mean much to the collector. It is fun doing the collecting and the collector has something to share with friends.

There are other collections we can make too that have a value we can never really measure. It is fun doing the collecting and they add a richness of experience to our lives that can be shared in many ways. Here are some ideas for such collections:

1. *Try collecting smiles.* Try it for just one day at first. You'll be so pleased with your collection that you'll want to keep right on collecting. Of course to collect smiles you have to smile at others first. You start with the first person you see when you get up in the morning and you keep right on through the day. Sometimes people will not give you a smile. Maybe they're too tired, or worried, or sick. Or maybe they're just so surprised at seeing you smile that they don't respond right away. But if you keep right on trying, sooner or later you'll get some kind of smile for your collection. And often the smile that's hardest to get will be the one you prize the most.

2. *Try collecting something beautiful each day*—not something you can put in a scrapbook or on a bulletin board, but something you can file away in your memory, something you can turn to and enjoy when things are going badly or that you can enjoy in moments of quiet. If you have a true collector's eye you'll find all sorts of things—tiny frost crystals on windows, the lace of bare black branches against a red sunset, tall grasses shimmering in the sun, white clouds reflected in the pond. There is a wealth of beauty around us just waiting to be collected.

3. *Collect a beautiful sound each day.* It could be a redbird's song in the dead of winter, or it could be the soft lap-lap of waves on the shore in summer. It might be the high clear notes of the meadow lark over the wheat fields, or it might be the symphony of insect sounds that you hear only when you're very quiet and listen very closely. Sort out the beautiful sounds from the ones you've grown accustomed to—cars on the highway, airplanes overhead, a radio or television going full blast. Sort them out and store them away. There will be many times when you can turn to your collection and enjoy it.

The earth is the Lord's and the fulness thereof,
the world and those who dwell therein . . .
O give thanks to the Lord, for he is good;
for his steadfast love endures for ever!
(Ps. 24:1; 106:1*b*)

I give thanks for the beauty that is all about me, Father. Keep me alert to the beauty of a smiling face, to the beauty of sights and sounds. Help me capture these moments of beauty and to remember that these are your gifts to enrich my life. AMEN.

when you try to understand . . .

The Other Fellow

DO YOU EVER STOP DURING THE DAY AND JUST WONDER about people around you—wonder what they're thinking, what they are wishing for, what they are really like inside where nobody can see?

President Garfield one time bowed very politely to a newsboy who sold him a paper, and then explained to his puzzled companion, "No one knows who's buttoned up in that jacket!"

No one knows—really knows—what is going on in another person's mind and heart.

Since there is always some deep part of another person that we can't feel or see or know, it is easy for us to misunderstand and misjudge our friends. That snub last week may not really have been a snub at all. Maybe it came because someone was having it tough getting his grades up to par, or because he was in trouble at home. The last time you had a quarrel with Mom—are you sure it was just because Mom didn't understand, or could it be that *you* didn't understand? Was Mom extra tired? Had things gone wrong at home all day? Was she disappointed that Dad couldn't get home for supper?

You never know, do you?

If we were just a little wiser, we would know that others need understanding just as much as we do. We usually find lots of good excuses for the foolish things *we* do. Usually there are good excuses for the foolish things *others* do too.

But our understanding of others must not depend alone on a good excuse! Those around us who act in ways we do not like—ways that sometimes hurt us—need our understanding even more when they act spitefully and have no "good excuse."

Bear one another's burdens, and so fulfil the law of Christ (GAL. 6:2).

O God, help me understand.
Help me understand . . .
when my friends ignore or hurt me . . .
when my family doesn't understand . . .
when everyone around me seems against me. . . .
Help me to help them. . .
loving my friends so they will know I understand . . .
loving my parents so that they will know I care, and forgive . . .
showing all who are against me that I will continue to love them until they can learn to love again. . . .
I thank thee . . .
for friends who understand me when I am weak . . .
for thy forgiveness of my foolish ways . . .
for thy understanding that helps me regain my love when I have been forgiven by thee. . . .
In Jesus' name I pray. AMEN.

We who have strong faith ought to shoulder the burden of the doubts and qualms of others and not just to go our own sweet way. Our actions should mean the good of others—should help them to build up their characters.
(ROM. 15:1-2 Phillips)

ever ask yourself . . .

What's My Line?

THIS MATTER OF TALENT, OR SPECIAL ABILITIES, OR whatever you want to call them, is one that often disturbs us. So often we say, "If I could only sing the way Mary does!" Or, "If I could only play basketball the way Charley does!" "If only . . ."

Has it ever occurred to you that even though you're not a nightingale like Mary, the chances are that there is probably something you can do as well or better than she does? You may not be able to hold a candle to Jack in basketball, but it's entirely possible that he would give a lot to be able to do something that you can do well.

Often we underestimate our own abilities when we rate them only in terms of what someone else can do. We forget that each of us is an individual personality, that each of us has unique talents and abilities unlike those of any other person in the world.

Maybe your talents or abilities have not been developed. Maybe you haven't even discovered what they are. But in serious thought and prayer not only can you discover them, you can find help for developing them.

Do you remember the story of God commanding Moses to tell the Pharaoh that he must let the Israelites leave Egypt? Moses was sure he couldn't be a diplomat; he compared himself with the flashy, capable men of the court. But even though Moses was not a good speaker, God knew that he was a great leader. So he sent Aaron to help Moses speak before the Pharaoh in order that Moses' great gift of leadership would not be lost.

But the Lord spoke to Moses and Aaron, and gave them a charge to the people of Israel and to Pharaoh king of Egypt to bring the people of Israel out of the land of Egypt. (EXOD. 6:13)

Spend some of your quiet time today thinking about your own talents and abilities. How can they be developed? How can you make the best use of them?

O God, show me how to discover my own special talents and abilities. Help me in evaluating what I can do —neither low-rating myself or overestimating my abilities. Lead me as I try to make the most of my talents and show me how to use them as you would have them used.

AMEN

when someone needs you, . . .

Are You Ready to Help?

HAVE YOU HEARD OF THE BOY WITH TWO UMBRELLAS?

He was a college student, still in his teens. On the first week of school, one night, he dropped into the dormitory across from his own and knocked on the door of a new law student, a young man from the Philippine Islands.

He simply wanted to welcome the new fellow, he said, and offer to help in any way he could. Before leaving, he asked what church his new friend went to. He found out that although his new friend was Christian, he did not go to church very much. "Well," said the young student, "I'll draw you a map and show you how to get to your church. It's on the other side of town, and you'd have a time finding it by yourself." So he drew the map and left.

Sunday morning came—rain, rain, rain. The Filipino waked up and saw the terrible weather. "Oh, no," he complained, "I can't go looking for my church in this awful weather. I just won't make it today!" And he turned over to catch some more sleep.

But there was a knock at the door.

There stood his new friend, who had drawn the map. He had on a raincoat, and on his arm were *two* umbrellas! "I knew you couldn't make it to church alone in this weather, so I've come to bring you an umbrella, and to show you the way to your church." So they sloshed out together into the downpour.

They had not gone far when the Filipino realized he had not bothered to ask about his friend's church. "Why, my church is just around the corner here," his guide said.

Then the foreign student decided that he would like to find out more about his friend's church. "Suppose," he said, "you and I go to your church today. Next week we can go to mine." And so they did. The visitor was so impressed by the sincerity of his guide that he soon decided to stay in the church of his friend. Finally, he found so much strength in the sincerity of his friend, and in the fellowship of the congregation his friend had taken him to, that he decided he ought to become a minister. He went on to seminary to study theology and before long returned to his land. Later, when he became Bishop Valencia of The Methodist Church in the Philippines, he liked to tell about the strange boy with the two umbrellas, who had made such a difference in his life.[2]

Now who would think of keeping two umbrellas—just in case someone needed help?

But that is the kind of thinking we need to do. We need to be ready to help, when the time comes. Oh, we may not actually carry two umbrellas on rainy days and our simple helpfulness may not change the life of a person so that he becomes a bishop. But we can be ready to help a new church member get into our group. Or we can go out of our way to make friends with the new girl or the new boy who has come into our room at school. And we can seek out new ways to help our sisters and brothers, or our parents.

As Christians, we want to be aware of the needs of persons around us. And we want to be ready to help them, for we know that God loves them, just as he loves us.

Think about this description of Jesus' life and of the purpose of his disciples:

. . . he went about doing good
and God was with him. (Acts 10:38)

Think today about persons you know who have special needs:

. . . about someone who does not have many friends.

. . . about someone in your family who needs your help.

. . . about a stranger in your town, whom you might help.

Decide now how you will help them. And then pray that God will help you carry out your plans.

see yourself . . .

From Another Angle

THE GREAT FRENCH PAINTER MONET PAINTED A PICture of a haystack thirty-two times—each time in a different degree of light. No two pictures were the same. Each portrayed the same haystack but the angle from which it was painted and the way the light fell gave it a different appearance in each one.

Sometimes when we are trying to grow as Christians it is good to remember Monet's haystack. Today we think we can tell pretty surely what being a Christian means. We try to do what we think we should and we try to keep from doing the things we believe are unchristian. Then tomorrow we read a book, we listen to a speech, we see some person giving himself away to help another, and we realize that we were seeing only a small part of the truth. Another day as we read our Bibles and spend some time in prayer and meditation we catch another glimmer of what it means to be a disciple of Jesus.

As long as we are sincerely trying to grow as Christians we will see our actions, our beliefs, or relationships with others and with God from a different angle each day. Today we get a bit more light here, tomorrow a bit more there. Sometimes it may seem that there is no change at all and we may become discouraged. On those days when it seems you are farther than ever from your goal as a Christian you can remember the haystack and the great painter who was always alert to the changing light.

Everyone who tries to live as a Christian has to change and grow. The apostle Paul had a good bit of growing up to do in his thinking and attitudes toward others when he decided to become a Christian. The advice he wrote to his friends in the church at Corinth shows how he was seeing life in a different light:

Our knowledge is imperfect . . . but when the perfect comes, the imperfect will pass away. When I was a child, I spoke like a child, I thought like a child, I reasoned like a child; when I became a man, I gave up childish ways. (I Cor. 13:9-11)

Guide me, Father, as I try to find a way of life that is truly Christian. Keep my mind open, ready to accept new learning and new understandings. Give me the wisdom and the courage to change my beliefs and my behavior as I grow in understanding. Amen.

Getting Along in a Group

LOTS OF PEOPLE—BOTH TEENAGERS AND GROWN-UPS—don't know too much about how to get along in the groups they belong to. But we spend a good bit of our time in groups, in clubs, in committees, and in Sunday school and youth groups at church. Perhaps we ought to try to understand what it means to be a good member of a group.

First of all, it means giving up a little of our independence. And that is not always pleasant. We like to run our own lives. But just as soon as we begin to take part in a group, we find that there are others who also like to run things! And something has to give. In a good group, everyone gives. No one insists that he has to have his way. But everybody takes part in decisions when the group has to make up its mind Sometimes we all agree in the end. But sometimes we don't.

And this means that in a group you have to agree to disagree. If you don't, the group will fall apart as soon as the first decision has to be reached. You may have been in a group that lasted only that long. But if you agree to disagree, you expect everyone to express his opinion and you know that everybody won't think alike. Thus, each person can be himself, and this makes an exciting group.

Each member of a group has to play his part. When

some members hold back and don't take part the whole group slows down. But when each person feels free to be himself and to share himself with the group, then the group is enriched, and things begin to move. This sort of group gives a person a place to express his ideas without being afraid of being laughed at. Here he has no fear that others will think he is strange or different. Each member of the group helps other members to grow.

Out of this kind of atmosphere there comes a harmony that is more valuable than simple agreement. When we learn to live with others happily, even when we disagree with them, and when we help each other to grow and mature in our thinking and attitudes, then there is a unity among us that nothing can break.

This is the unity the psalmist talked about:

Behold, how good and pleasant it is
when brothers dwell in unity!
It is like the precious oil upon the head,
running down upon the beard,
upon the beard of Aaron,
running down on the collar of his robes!
It is like the dew of Hermon,
which falls on the mountains of Zion!
For there the Lord has commanded the blessing,
life for evermore. (Ps. 133)

O God, since the groups I belong to are so important to me, help me to learn how to play my part in them. I want to learn how to understand the viewpoints of the others; I want to know how to give in when others are right; I want to learn to be myself in every group I belong to, and to find out ways to dwell together in unity with all of the people who belong to the groups I do. In Jesus' name I pray. AMEN.

when you go . . .

Below the Surface

EXCITING THINGS ARE HAPPENING NOWADAYS DEEP under the surface of the ocean. New developments in diving equipment and devices for underwater exploration are making it possible to discover all sorts of treasures. Ships that went down centuries ago are being located and their cargoes brought to the surface. A sculptured urn, rescued from the deep and identified by experts as the work of certain ancient craftsmen, adds to our knowledge of past arts. A battleship that has been lying in the ocean for hundreds of years supplies a missing piece of history's jigsaw. Ancient coins tell of kings and governments dead long ago. A sample of the ocean floor itself speaks eloquently to the geologist, and specimens of marine life from the blue-green world thousands of feet down under yield their secrets to the naturalist. Below the waves that shine and foam and toss on its surface the ocean holds more treasures than we can possibly imagine.

Yes, hidden from our view is a fabulous wealth. Only the daring ones, only those who are willing take a great risk, dare to dive beneath the surface and find what is there.

In our friendships it's much the same. We so seldom see below the surface, so seldom find the real treasures in another's personality. Rather we accept persons as our friends for what they appear to be. John laughs a lot, so we accept him as a jolly person. But beneath that laughter, if we went that deep, we might discover a very serious person—a person who could share his deep thoughts and who could become a wonderful friend. We label Mary as a snob because she appears to be so cold and distant. But if we went below the surface we might discover that May is a very warm, friendly person who wants very much to be a friend. But because she isn't quite sure of herself, she covers up her shyness with what seems to be snobbishness. We describe a teacher as an ogre, we call parents dictators. Yet, if we went beneath the surface we might find very good reasons for these adults to behave as they do. And in discovering these, we might also discover rich treasures in friendship and understanding.

Why is it we will not risk going below the surface in our relationships with others? Are we unwilling to give a little extra effort, a little extra time, a little bit of ourselves to find the treasures in others' personalities—the treasures that lie below the surface?

Think about your friendships today. Are they mostly of the surface variety? Or, are you making an effort to go below the surface, to discover the real treasures in the personalities of your friends?

Get wisdom, and whatever you get, get insight. . . .
(PROV. 4:7)

O God, I know that I often accept others only for what I see on the surface. Help me to go deeper, to find the rich treasures in their personalities—the treasures than can mean rich relationships and deep, warm friendships. AMEN.

when you ask yourself . . .

Why Should I Help?

SOMETIMES IT IS HARD TO GO OUT OF OUR WAY TO HELP someone. We are tired, or angry, or confused—and it just doesn't seem right that we should strain ourselves to help somebody else. Why should we, when we don't feel like it?

There is a simple answer to that question. It is found in a story Jesus told his disciples a couple of days before he was arrested. Jesus was imagining what the end of the world will be like and he tells about the King who will speak to all men—those who have pleased him, and those who have not. To those who have pleased him, he says:

"Come, O blessed of my Father, inherit the kingdom prepared for you from the foundation of the world; for I was hungry and you gave me food, I was thirsty and you gave me drink, I was a stranger and you welcomed me, I was naked and you clothed me, I was sick and you visited me. I was in prison and you came to me." Then the righteous will answer him, "Lord, when did we see thee hungry and feed thee, or thirsty and give thee drink? And when did we see thee a stranger and welcome thee, or naked and clothe thee? And when did we see thee sick or in prison and visit thee?" And the king will answer them, "Truly, I say to you, as you did it to one of the least of these my brethren, you did it to me."

(MATT. 25:34-40)

There is the answer Jesus gave to the question, "Why should I help other people, even when I don't feel like it?" In helping them, you are serving him.

Should your feelings determine how you act? Are you supposed to love others only when it is convenient—only when it makes you feel good?

When you realize that Christ is present in the person

who needs your help, aren't you encouraged to serve more faithfully—even if you don't feel like it?

O God, help me to see thee in every person I meet. Show me ways to be of help to each person—the stranger, the prisoner, the hungry, the thirsty—and give me strength to do the things you show me to do. In Jesus' name. AMEN.

maybe what you want is just . . .

Cotton Candy

HAVE YOU EVER WATCHED A COTTON CANDY MACHINE? How fascinating it is to see that pink and blue and purple film spin round and round. How exciting it is to watch the white-aproned man gather that loveliness into a cone with a few expert twists.

But what a disappointment when you try to eat it! Immediately that beautiful fluffiness dissolves into nothing at all—no substance, no taste, only a stickiness that somehow gets all over your face and hands.

When we find ourselves wanting something very much we might be wise to remind ourselves of cotton candy. For example, suppose you want more than anything else to belong to a certain group. You give up time that you know should be spent in study, or in practicing, or in making worthwhile friendships. Maybe you spend more money than you know you can afford trying to buy your way in. It is even possible that your standards might be lowered or ideals set aside. Will popularity achieved that way really be worth all your effort? Or, will it turn out like the cotton candy—something that melts into nothingness?

How about that new dress or the new shoes that you're willing to spend everything for today? Or the invitation to that party that seems almost of life-or-death importance? Or the date that you think will once-and-for-all make you one of the "inside" crowd?

It is easy to look back and see where many of the things we wanted so much in the past were not really worth our efforts. It is not so easy to look ahead and see how we may feel tomorrow about what seems important today. But we can try to think through. We can honestly try to determine whether there are real and lasting values in what we want. We can learn by past mistakes. For all this is a part of growing up, a part of becoming mature in our thinking and living. Only as we learn to control and direct our thoughts and our physical energies can we hope to become either truly Christian or truly adult.

When I was a child, I spoke like a child, I thought like a child, I reasoned like a child; when I became a man, I

gave up childish ways. . . . Examine yourselves, to see whether you are holding to your faith. Test yourselves. Do you not realize that Jesus Christ is in you?

(I Cor. 13:11; II Cor. 13:5)

O God, help me examine carefully the things I want most. Guide me as I test them in the light of Jesus' life and teachings. Show me the way to outgrow childishness in my reasoning and in my choices. AMEN.

before you decide you can't, . . .

Give It a Try!

"BUT WHY SHOULD I TRY? I KNOW I CAN'T."

Have you said that lately? About trying to make the team at school? Or about writing a poem? About leading a class discussion or making a report?

Most of us have felt that there are things that we just cannot do, and often we get in the rut of saying "I can't." All will be going along just fine for us, when we find ourselves faced with a new task. "I can't do it," we say, almost without thinking.

The prophet Elijah, strong and influential as he was, said it one day. His king was chasing him because he had destroyed all the pagan priests. He ran until he couldn't run any more, and sat down to rest under a tree.

"It is enough; now, O Lord, take away my life; for I am no better than my fathers." And he lay down and slept . . . and behold, an angel touched him, and said to him, "Arise and eat." And he looked, and behold, there was at his head a cake baked on hot stones and a jar of water. And he ate and drank, and lay down again. And the angel of the Lord came again a second time, and touched him and said, "Arise and eat, else the journey will be too great for you." And he arose, and ate and drank, and went in the strength of that food forty days and forty nights to Horeb the Mount of God.

(I Kings 19:4-8)

Elijah said, "I can't." But he found out that he could keep going, and he did. We need to think seriously about the times we say "I can't." We need to do our best to *try* to do the hard things we face. Trying is important for several reasons.

For one thing, trying helps us find out what we *can* do. You can probably remember times when you first found out you were able to do something—jump off the high diving board, or spell Mississippi. From then on, you knew you could. And you did.

For another thing, trying helps us know what we *cannot* do. And this is just as important to us as knowing what we can do. When we know what our limits are, we do not spend our time in frustrating activities. If your hand won't reach an octave on the piano, for example, it would be silly for you to plan to be a concert pianist, wouldn't it?

So you see that trying helps us find out what we really can and cannot do. In other words, it helps us know what role we can play in life. In the process of "keeping on"—failing sometimes and succeeding sometimes—we gradually develop skills that lead us in the direction of our life's work.

O God, help me to be honest with myself when I have to try to do hard things. When I fail in them, show me how to learn from my failure. When I succeed, encourage me to try something harder. And help me to learn to know the difference between what I really cannot do, and what—by trying—I can do. AMEN.

don't forget that . . .

You Can Depend on God

TAKE TIME TODAY TO THINK ABOUT THIS DEPENDABLE old world of ours.

Think about the seasons of the year, to begin with. It never occurs to you that spring might follow summer this year, does it? You know that spring is going to follow winter and that summer is going to follow spring and that autumn and winter will be coming after summer. How wonderfully dependable the seasons are!

Think about the great forces in the physical world—the force of gravity, for example. You know for certain that wherever you stand on this globe the force of gravity will keep you from floating off into space. You know too that anything you drop will fall to the ground or the floor. You can be sure that anything you throw into the air—whether it's a tiny pebble or an inflated football—will come back to earth. What a wonderful law that makes it possible for us to be so sure of all this!

And, think about the stars there in the sky. The North Star will be in its place night after night. The Great Bear, or Big Dipper, will swing to its seasonal position year after year. You know you will be able to see the Milky Way on any clear night. You can depend on the laws that control the stars.

Or think about the sun. Maybe you can't see it every day because of the clouds, but you know it is there and, as our planet turns in space, it provides the light for our days. And the moon—we know for a certainty how the little new moon will appear, how it will pass through the various stages until it becomes a bright, full moon. Think of the tides, or the cycle of birth, growth, and death in all of nature.

There are laws at work here and throughout our universe that we can be very sure about, that we can depend on. And all this brings us finally to God, the Creator, the one who set our universe and all the other universes spinning away in space, the one who set up these laws that we can depend on. What a great God this is—how loving, how just, how dependable!

For ever, O Lord, thy word
is fixed firmly in the heavens.
Thy faithfulness endures to all generations;
thou hast established the earth, and it stands fast . . .
O give thanks to the Lord,
for he is good;
his steadfast love endures for ever!
(Ps. 119:89-90; 118:1)

Father, forgive me when I forget that your dependable laws govern our world. Forgive me too when I fail to remember that these laws are laws of love basic to my security and well-being. Remind me often to recognize the operation of these dependable laws when I think things are going wrong in the world. I pray in Jesus' name. AMEN.

knowing how to make friends is . . .

A Secret Worth Telling

I know sumpin' I'm not gonna tell;
Two little boys in a peanut shell.
One can read, and one can write,
And one won't go to sleep at night.

SOME SECRETS ARE NOT WORTH TELLING, ARE THEY? But some are. We are going to try to discover a real secret today: how to make friends.

All of us talk about making new friends. Sometimes we even worry because we do not have more friends, or as many as we want. What we do not know is that there is a simple way to solve our problem.

But before you hear what it is, it will help if you will read what Jesus told one of the scribes who asked him who his neighbor was:

Jesus replied, "A man was going down from Jerusalem to Jericho, and he fell among robbers, who stripped him and beat him, and departed, leaving him half-dead. Now by chance a priest was going down that road; and when he saw him he passed by on the other side. So likewise a Levite, when he came to the place and saw him passed by on the other side. But a Samaritan, as he journeyed, came to where he was; and when he saw him, he had compassion, and went to him and bound up his wounds, pouring on oil and wine; then he set him on his own beast and brought him to an inn, and took care of him.

And the next day he took out two denarii and gave them to the innkeeper, saying. 'Take care of him; and whatevery more you spend, I will repay you when I come back.' Which of these three, do you think, proved neighbor to the man who fell among the robbers?"

(LUKE 10:30-36)

The kind of person Jesus was talking about in this parable is the kind of person everyone would want for a friend. Just think—he would always be trying to do what is right, with everything he had. He would always be thinking about the other fellow in the same ways he thinks about himself. He would be doing to others what he wants them to do to him.

He would have more friends than he would know what to do with. Everyone would want him to help them with their problems. When he grew up, all kinds of jobs would open up for him, and he would mean something to his whole community.

You would certainly like to have him for a friend, I know.

And do you know something else? If *you* try to become that person, trying to follow Christ's way in your own life, you will find that many people will want you for a friend. *That's the only secret there is to making friends. A long time ago it was put in this wise little sentence: To make a friend, you must first be one!*

That is right—if you want a lot of friends, then you

must be sure that you are becoming the kind of person others will want for a friend. *Now you know.*

O God, help me to be the kind of person who is a friend to all. Help me learn to love thee completely, and to love all my friends with fairness. AMEN.

for days when you ask yourself . . .

Where Do I Stand?

DURING A RECENT TELEVISION SHOW A COMEDIAN turned to the director offstage and asked, "Now where do I stand?" With appropriate wisecracks he found the mark on the floor that indicated his position for the next scene.

If we could have watched rehearsals for the show we would have seen how important it was that the actor stand on the right mark. Where he stood made a difference to the camera man who must get just the right angle. It made a difference in the quality of the picture we saw on our screens for the lighting had been carefully tested at that spot; make-up and costumes had been checked in that lighting. It made a difference in the sound, for microphones had been placed to pick up his voice at that exact point. And it made a big difference to the other actors. If he did not stand on his mark it meant that they could not stand where they were supposed to.

No wonder he stopped the show to ask, "Where do I stand?" It was essential that he stand in the right place!

Sometimes we, too, have to pause and ask, "Where do I stand?" Every day we have many experiences which demand that we take a stand, that we show by our speech or action what that stand is. Unlike the television actor, we do not have clearly marked places on which to stand. For us, it is a matter of finding where we must stand and this takes thoughtful effort. There are times when we must find a place to be alone to rethink experiences and conversations. We have to recall what we have read, what teachers and friends and parents have said about some particular question. Again, we have to call on others to help us as we try to find where we stand. And often we must turn to God and to the Bible for guidance.

In these quiet moments today think about where you stand. Ask yourself:

Where do I stand when someone is being "taken apart" by the crowd?

Where do I stand when the actions of the crowd do not square with what I think is right?

Where do I stand when I am tempted to lie, or cheat, or steal?

Where do I stand on any special question that is bothering me today?

The place on which you are standing is holy ground . . . God is our refuge and strength, a very present help in trouble. **(EXOD. 3:5; PS. 46:1)**

Father, help me to pause often and ask, "Where do I stand?" Guide me in thinking through to right answers. Strengthen me to stand firmly when I have found the place to stand. Forgive me when I take a wrong stand, but give me courage to admit that I have been wrong and to try harder to find the right place to stand. AMEN.

when you wonder . . .

All About Dating!

SOMETIMES WE THINK AND WORRY SO MUCH ABOUT dating we forget to *enjoy* our dates.

There are so many questions. How late can I stay out? Shouldn't I be able to take the car? Why chaperons at parties? Kissing? What else—and how far?

There's no question about there being plenty of questions, is there? And you would like answers to all of them? There are answers to each and every question you and your friends come up with. But those answers are not in any book anywhere. They are your answers, and you will have to find them for yourself. Sorry. No short cuts to "the right way" here.

But there are helps.

There are friends to talk with: your parents, your teachers, your minister, and other adults with whom you feel you can talk.

There are good books to read. Your teachers at school and at church will help you choose good ones.

And there is your own commitment to Christ. In every relationship of your life, you are trying to apply the principle of love. You try it in your life at school and at home, and in your recreation. You must apply it to dating too.

How?

Well—start by finding out how love acts:

Love is patient and kind; love is not jealous or boastful; it is not arrogant or rude. Love does not insist on its own way; it is not irritable or resentful; it does not rejoice at wrong, but rejoices in the right. Love bears all things, believes all things, hopes all things, endures all things. (I Cor. 13:4-7)

There is the picture of the love the Christian tries to show.

No *rules,* you see. But a challenge to learn to be loving in all these ways, a challenge to *climb* into love, rather than falling into it! Then dating takes its proper place along with other happy parts of your life as a Christian.

You forget the sweat about the rules and the right and wrong. You relax, and enjoy the evening.

And that, after all, is just what God wants you to do. In love, of course.

O God, teach me what true love is. Help me realize that the love Christ gives is much deeper and more satisfying than what many of my friends call "love." In all of my life, and especially in my dating, may I show the love that Christ has shown me. And in the time that you have chosen, lead me into the bonds of deep love that will bring me to marriage and the founding of my own home. In the name of Christ. AMEN.

for a day when you're ...

Not in the Mood

"I'M JUST NOT IN THE MOOD TO WRITE LETTERS TODAY—or play the piano—or go to town—or—" Ever say something like that? Or like this:

"I know I should have congratulated him, but I was in a mean mood." . . . "I shouldn't have spent all my allowance, but I was in a spending mood." . . . "I had a deep blue mood and just didn't speak."

Let's take a look at these moods. Are we being entirely honest in saying we do or do not do a thing because of a certain mood? Could it be that sometimes a mood is an excuse for not doing something we don't want to do, or for doing something we know we shouldn't do?

Could it be, too, that we sometimes pretend to be in a mood in order to get what we want from others? "Poor John (or Mary) is in a low mood today!" becomes sweet music and tells us parents or friends will give us their special consideration. So we take advantage of their concern and love to make a selfish request.

We cannot deny the fact that we are all moody at times. But an explanation of our actions entirely in terms of those moods isn't very grown up, is it? What if your mother explained that she didn't prepare dinner because she just wasn't in the mood? What if your father didn't go to work today for the same reason? What would happen to farm crops and farm animals if farmers took care of them only when in the mood? What if—ridiculous, you say!

Yes, it is ridiculous. A part of growing up, of becoming an adult personality is learning to control our moods, learning to take ourselves in hand (even when it's hard) and go ahead with what needs doing.

Sometimes the mood changes as we do this. A deep blue mood may turn to a lighter shade. Sometimes it changes colors completely as we forget ourselves and bring happiness to others. At other times we may not be able to shake a mood entirely, but we can work at it and there's a wonderful sense of achievement as we discover that we're making progress.

All moods, of course, are not bad ones. There are the happy joyful moods too and we can certainly make the most of these. We find that they come more often as we learn to control the ugly ones. Pausing to remember that we live in a world where God loves each of us, his children, and understands us whatever our mood may be, gives us strength to work at dispelling the bad moods and deepens the joy of our happy moods.

Blessed are those who hunger and thirst for righteousness, for they shall be satisfied. . . . Be strong, and let your heart take courage. . . . Look to him and be radiant.
(Matt. 5:6; Ps. 27:14; 34:5)

Father, guide me and strengthen me as I try to become an adult. Help me as I work at overcoming bad moods and show me how to stretch out the happy ones into a deep and abiding joy. I know that I live each day in the security of your love and understanding, but help me always to remember this. Amen.

don't settle for less than . . .

A Brand New World!

THE COWBOY HAD BEEN QUITE A GUY. ALL OVER HIS section of the territory, he was known as a tough fighter and a fast man with a gun. You stayed out of his way unless you wanted trouble. But one night the cowboy went to a tent revival, and was converted.

Several weeks later he rode into town, and his horse knowing his habits, took him straight to the saloon. The cowboy hopped off and threw the reins around the hitching rail. Just then the preacher came by. "If you're gonna follow Jesus, cowboy," he said, "you'll hafta find yourself a new hitching rail!"

When we decide we are going to live our lives as Christ directs, we have to find ourselves new hitching posts, too. Becoming a Christian makes everything new for us.

We begin to see the world through new eyes! Before, the world was just the place we happened to inhabit. But when we hear what Christ has to say about life, we realize that this world is God's. We know that it is good and that it offers a good life to us.

We see the people around us in a new light! Before, they just happened to be around: one day, they were helpful to us; the next day, they were problems. But when we begin to live as Christ's followers, we discover that the people around us are all God's children, and that he has called us to love them into loving him.

And we even see ourselves as brand new—almost as if we hadn't ever seen ourselves before. For now we begin to understand ourselves. We know that God has a purpose in creating us. We know that he has a plan for us in his bright, challenging world. We know that we belong to him, and that he is our Father.

When God helps us to see these things, then we know that the old way of seeing and knowing and living won't do any more. We begin to look for a new hitching rail, a new place to tie up while we go about the business of every day.

Paul has good advice for us:

Give your heart to the heavenly things, not to the passing things of earth. . . . Have nothing to do with sexual immorality, dirty-mindedness, uncontrolled passion, evil desire, and the lust for other people's goods, which last, remember, is as serious a sin as idolatry. It is because of these very things that the holy anger of God falls upon those who refuse to obey him. And never forget that you had your part in those dreadful things when you lived that old life.

But now, put all these things behind you. No more evil temper or furious rage: no more evil thoughts or words about others, no more evil thoughts or words about God, and no more filthy conversation. Don't tell one another lies any more, for you have finished with the old man and all he did and have begun a life as a new man, who is out

to learn what he ought to be, according to the plan of God. (Col. 3:2, 5-10 Phillips)

Today pray that God will help you see everything around you in a fresh, new way—his way. Ask him to help you understand the world, and your friends, and yourself. Seek his purpose for your life, and commit yourself to it.

Prayers

In the Morning

Let me hear in the morning of thy steadfast love,
for in thee I put my trust.
Teach me the way I should go,
for to thee I lift up my soul.[3]

AMEN.

For This Day

Today, O Lord—
let me put right before interest:
let me put others before self:
let me put the things of the spirit before the things of the body:
let me put the attainment of noble ends above the enjoyment of present pleasures:
let me put principle above reputation:
let me put Thee before all else.[4]

AMEN.

In the Evening

Now unto thee, O heavenly Father, be all praise and glory that day by day Thou dost richly fill my life with various blessings:

A home to share, kindred to love, and friends to cherish:
A place to fill and work to do:
A green world to live in, blue skies above me, and pure air to breathe:
Healthy exercise and simple pleasures:
My race's long history to remember and its great men to follow:
Good books to read and many arts and crafts to delight in:
So much that is worth knowing and the skill and science to know it:
Those high thoughts that sometimes fill my mind and come I know not whence:
Many happy days, and that inward calm that Thou givest me in days of gloom:
The peace, passing understanding, that comes from Thine indwelling in my soul:
The faith that looks through death and the hope of a larger life beyond the grave.

AMEN.[5]

For My Family

O God, our Father, bless my family. Guide us as we learn to live together in love, as thou hast commanded us.

Accept my thanks:

for the warmth and security I find at home with those who love me.

for opportunities to grow in favor with thee as I honor my parents.

for the great truths thou dost show me as I see the love of my parents for each other and for me.

for the chance I have to live my life as an example to others in my home.

for the forgiveness my family shows when I fall short of their expectation for me.

for the ways in which my home is open to others, who find love and understanding and security there.

Help me always to cherish the love thou hast given me in my home. In the name of Christ I pray. AMEN.

For My School and My Teachers

O God, show me the importance of my school days. Help me to realize that even in these days of preparation, you are calling me to serve you, and that my desk can be my altar.

Help me to appreciate the love and helpfulness shown to me by my teachers and my classmates. When they are impatient, let me be forgiving; and when I treat them with disrespect, let me seek their forgiveness—and thine. And let me always be aware of the task we have together—to find your Truth, that we may be free men and women.

In Christ's name I pray. AMEN.

Before Examinations

O God, be with me today and help me to do my best. Give me a clear mind and an honest heart. If there are things I do not know, let me not be flustered or afraid, but use to the utmost what I do know. May everything in which I have worked hard stand by me now; and if in anything I must face the results of laziness, make me resolve to work better in the days ahead. Help me to express all I know; but whether I can do that or not, grant that I may have learned something that will last; through Jesus Christ my Master. AMEN.[6]

For My Friends and Neighbors

O thou who art the God of all the families of the earth, bless, I pray Thee, all our friends and neighbors. Watch over their homes and shield them from all harm and evil. Protect their dwellings from fire, from thieves, and from anything that would destroy them or bring them trouble. Help me to be thoughtful for their welfare and the protection of their property. Show me how I can serve them. Make me a ready and willing friend and a true neighbor. For Jesus' sake. AMEN.[7]

For a Friend in Sorrow

O God, while my friend is in sorrow over the loss of one very dear, help me show true friendship. Help me be quiet and understanding when I should; and give me words to speak when I feel that something should be said. Let my love, and the warmth of my own home, help to heal the sadness in his heart.

Guide him through these days, so that he may remember your love for him and find the reassurance he needs to face his everyday tasks again.

Through Christ, our Lord. AMEN.

For Good Leaders

Almighty God, send us brave and clear thinkers to lead us; give them courage and boldness to fight for the best and highest, and help us all to give them our sincere and thoughtful support. AMEN.[8]

For a Better World

O Thou who art the Father of us all, reveal unto us the things we can do to free the world from oppression and to bring justice to all people, regardless of race, color, or creed. Grant that we may have a real concern for those we have previously ignored or neglected. Forgive us for our indifference toward the suffering of others, and for our selfishness which blinds us to the needs of those about us. Grant that we may do all in our power to hasten the day when the exploited and the weak, the backward and the downtrodden, will have an equal chance with those who are more favored. In the name of Jesus, we pray. AMEN.[9]

Before Attending a Service of Worship

O God, soon I will be with others worshiping you. Help me to come into your presence with sincere and high intentions, so that your Holy Spirit may speak, and I may find you.

May the prayers we pray together be the prayers of

true worshipers. May our hymns reflect the happiness we feel knowing that you are our God. May the meditations of our hearts as well as the words we speak lead us closer into fellowship with you and with each other. And may we hear the call to service that always comes when we have sought and found you, our heavenly Father.

In the name of Christ. AMEN.

For God's Love

O God, I thank thee for thy love that never ends. No matter how far short I fall of thy commands to me, I remember that thou still dost love me. I know that thy love is the foundation of my life. Without thee—without thy supporting and never-ending love—I cannot live.

I know that

neither death, nor life,
neither heavenly, nor earthly beings,
neither today's mistakes, nor tomorrow's troubles,
neither the lowest nor the highest powers that exist,
nor anything else in thy whole creation
can separate me from thy love.

I thank thee, O God; I thank thee. How can I accept so high and holy a gift?

In the name of Christ I pray. AMEN.[10]

For My Calling

Show me, O Lord, what my life's work is to be. Help me to find what I can do best and prepare me for it now in mind and body; through Jesus Christ our Lord. AMEN.[11]

Thankfulness for God's Care

O God, our Heavenly Father, Thou hast freely given us all things. Thou hast made the world beautiful. Thou dost send the sunshine and the rain that the earth may yield us food and flowers. Thou hast given us the homes we love, and hast set us among many friends. All day long we are safe in Thy keeping; and at night we sleep in peace because of Thy gracious care.

We thank Thee, our Father, for all these gifts of Thy bounty. As Thou dost love us, so may we, by loving and helping others, show ourselves Thy grateful children. AMEN.[12]

For Daily Guidance

O God, help me remember that all the happy moments of my life come as gifts from you, so that I my rejoice always in your love.

To you, I can come unafraid with all my requests, knowing that you will hear my prayer. I will not be anxious or fearful, for I know that you, who are the heavenly Father of all men, do love and keep me. The peace that I cannot understand will steady my heart and mind on the love of Christ, whose example I keep before me always.

Help me to think about the things that matter most in my life—whatever is true, whatever is honorable, whatever is just, whatever is pure, whatever is lovely, whatever is gracious. May your love strengthen me as I learn to live my life according to your excellent ways.

In the name of Christ, our Lord. AMEN.[13]

When I Fail

O God, I have failed.

I have failed you, and myself, and all those who love me and expect me to live according to my best.

I want to do my best always. Even when I do, though, I sometimes fail; help me accept my failures. But often I fail because I do not try hard enough and do not see the importance of being my best. Forgive me for my laziness and my neglect of what is important in my life.

Whenever I am weak but could be strong, forgive me. Whenever I am strong but not strong enough give me new strength through thy love. And when I am weak and cannot be stronger, help me accept my limits and learn to use the talents you have given me. In Jesus' name. AMEN.

For God's Presence

God be in my head, and in my understanding;
God be in my eyes, and in my looking;
God be in my mouth, and in my speaking;
God be in my heart, and in my thinking;
God be at mine end, and at my departing.[14]
AMEN.

For Humility

O Lord, who hast taught us that we can be forgiven only as we ourselves forgive: Help us ever to bear in mind our own shortcomings, so that when we remember the injuries we have suffered and never deserved, we may also remember the kindnesses we have received and never earned, and the punishments we have deserved but never suffered; that we may render unto thee our thanks for thy mercies, and for the mercies of our fellow men; for thy holy Name's sake.[15] AMEN.

For God's Will

May the strength of God pilot us.
May the power of God preserve us.
May the wisdom of God instruct us.
May the hand of God protect us.
May the way of God direct us.
May the shield of God defend us.
May the host of God guard us against the snares of the Evil One and the temptations of the world.
May Christ be with us. Christ before us.
Christ in us. Christ over us.
May thy salvation, O Lord, be always ours this day and for evermore.[16] AMEN.

Sources

1. "Valentine for Earth," by Frances Frost, from *Twelve/Fifteen*. Used by permission.
2. Story from Dr. Gordon Torgerson, First Baptist Church, Worcester, Massachusetts.
3. Ps. 143:8.
4. Reprinted with the permission of Oxford University Press and Charles Scribner's Sons from *A Diary of Private Prayer* by John Baillie, copyright 1949 Charles Scribner's Sons.
5. *Ibid.*, p. 103.
6. Walter Russell Bowie, *Lift Up Your Hearts* (Nashville: Abingdon Press), pp. 108-9. Used by permission.
7. From *Prayers for Boys*, by H. C. Alleman, Thomas Nelson & Sons.
8. M. L. Playfoot, *St. Francis Prayer Book* (Greenwich, Conn.: The Seabury Press). Used by permission.
9. Alice A. Bays, *Worship Programs and Stories for Young People* (Nashville: Abingdon Press), p. 101. Used by permission.
10. Based on Rom. 8:38-39.
11. *Service Book for Schools* (New York: The Macmillan Co.). Used by permission.
12. Hugh Hartshorne, *The Book of Worship of the Church School* (New York: Charles Scribner's Sons).
13. Based on Phil. 4:4-8.
14. Attributed to St. Patrick.
15. *A Collection of Prayers Used at Groton School.* Used by permission of the Headmaster, Groton School, Groton, Mass.
16. Attributed to St. Patrick.